Sunrise of Thought

Bruce A Humphrey

Print ISBN: 979-8-35097-101-9

Printed in the United States of America

Contents

Want or Will

How does a hungering child wait in silence before being fed?
How do a starving people continue to live?
How does a race of people have the will to fight perpetual torment?

How does a person needing friendship able to move forward?
How does a soul longing for love continue on?
How does a human thirsting for loyalty keep showing confidence?

How does an individual looking for trust wait for that one day?
How does a person who wants the truth wait against the lies?
How do people who are being oppressed endure an onslaught?

How do people use their hearts to help someone off the ground?
How do societies put aside differences to help the needy?
How do nations rise against evil and look skyward to help?

How do we know there is an answer?
How can a people realize the answer is not there?
How can a world know the future is never what it could be?

Tigers Talons

A tiger's eyes are narrowed.
He sees only prey.
Crouching behind peace, talons are readied.

Barriers begin to fall and the crouch becomes ruthless.
Fangs bare signaling the attack.
The prey moves closer, eyes fixed on their target.

People rise to halt the attack, but are stared into submission.
The tiger strikes and the talons slash.
They bow and die.

War is blind.
War ends when there is nothing.
Peace rises again.

Mortals

Mortals we are, mortal we remain.
Masters of our lives and masters of our lies.
Full of soulful thought yet unmoved by sorrow.

Lives we touch stir the mind.
People we hurt cast us backward.
But how we grieve keeps us alive.

Brothers, sisters, sons and daughters.
We live together but apart from all.
Fooling others fools ourselves.

As life moves onward it dwells in the past.
It does not learn however it learns as it grows.
Death does not teach; death is a passage to life.

The White Dove

The white dove of peace is lost in darkness.
Wandering aimlessly, it drifts in the blackness.
No points of light it sees as it searches for the light of hope.

Hope is fleeting in the darkness.
Tears fall from its bright eyes of faith.
It worries about the world.

It worries about life.
It worries about home.
Faith in the future keeps it soaring, searching.

Voices

Voices of billions.
Voices of people.
Life surrounds us.

The life of being.
Lives of the living.
Lives of the free to be.

Freedom sings.
Freedom, dreaming.
Do we live? Do we die?

Life graces life.
It grows as freedom grows.
Dreaming of life, the voices sing to the heavens.

A Day in June

A man, a boy, dies next to me.
In an instant he became silent.
A hole in his helmet was the final testament to his life.

A whistling of bullets and another drops to the sand.
A scream, another scream, but I must run onward.
Be brave, be quick, run, run, run to the cliff.

Explosion after explosion. I made it.
I look back at the sea. Bodies bob up and down in the water.
Dozens of bodies in the sand lie unmoving.

Small rivers of red flow away from my friends. The water has turned a faint red.
More crash to the sand. Some at my side, and others nearly make it but do not.
The sounds of explosions drown out the screams of the wounded.

I must be brave.
I must help my friends, my brothers.
I will move onward.

I shoot and shoot again.
Men I do not know, die.
I saved many of my brothers today.

It's over—the battle quiets.
I hear only the sounds of machines.
I sit and fumble weakly for some water.

I drink quickly and deeply.
I draw in a deep fresh breath.
In the distance, I can hear a pop and I sleep.

We are…

a species of savages.
a species made for war.
a species made of executioners.

fearful of other species.
fearful of losing to others.
fearful of loving.

afraid of living.
afraid of dying.
afraid of growing.

a species afraid of itself.
a species unsure of itself.
a species without the will to walk forward.

a species that is constantly looking for help.
a species that is continually changing.
a species that does evolve with each year that passes.

as we have always been.
as loving and compassionate as the rising sun.
as honorable and noble as a defiant mountain.

Brothers, Sisters, Sons, and Daughters

Our shadows are in one another.
We live and breathe as one.
Our hearts beat together.
A beat for a breath, a breath for each beat.

Paths of anger and love keep us together.
Distance is not a barrier, merely a bridge to a heart.
We talk to each other through our tearful eyes.
Eyes that have seen the trials and loves of life.

Playing together, laughing together.
Pride to see each other grow.
An extreme joy to see our families together.
Our children playing, adults talking freely.

Changing lives, changing directions pull on us.
Dragging us toward new destinies.
Leading us away from our childhoods.
Leading us to new callings, callings that touch our hearts.

But we do not forget.
We never fail to invoke the word, family.
Families that remember are families that are endless.
Endless in their family bonds that do not die.

But We Live On

Primal life to primal life.
We are who we are.
Changes to changes.
Unending to unending.

We are truthful to ourselves but are not.
We hate and love in the same breath.
We live and grow or wither and die.
All in the same direction as the wind.

Fighting or caressing the world.
At the same moment, we destroy and build.
Scaring ourselves and healing the future.
The future becomes the past and reverses.

Learning from the past but not changing the future.
Regressing towards the past while trying to live in the future.
The world becomes afraid of itself.
Terror comes to the forefront and directs our lives.

But we live on.
Turning around like the future and the past.
But we live on.
Marching forward and back in the same motion, but we live on.

Stand by Me

You will stand by me as I look down at you.
You look up at me.
Our teary eyes meet and you stand by me.

You stand by me through sickness and sorrow.
When happiness and joy envelop us.
When we create things together, you stand by me.

You stand by me as the sun rises and sets.
Through the darkness and light.
Our lives together will be forever because you stand by me.

Two

One meets another.
Eyes touch, love connects.
A love for years.

One walks with one.
Love grows.
One stands with the other.

Hopes, cares, and wishes become alive.
The future brightens.
The sun beams over the two.

One becomes two.
Two grow into one.
Two are now one for life.

Silence

Is a word that is seen and not said.
Is a feather fluttering to the earth.
Quiet as a seed of fluff that floats through the air.
Silence is louder than a cannon before a powerful army.

The blind knows the silence of the night.
The deaf knows the permanence of peace.
The mute knows the labor of a silent word.
An unspoken word of terror and delight.

Silence is a snowflake resting on a blade of grass.
Or a drop of water running down a window pane.
Silence is a massive tree birthing in the ground.
Or it is quiet as a lazy warm afternoon.

Silence is a malevolent thought.
A soul that is screaming in terror.
Or a thought of sublime love.
Glacial and serene as the sun quietly rises above the horizon.

Silence is a learning tool.
A learning that transcends time.
Silence is power.
A power that is both covert and truthful.

The Fountain

You cannot drink from my fountain.
It is mine, not for you. There will be no water for you.
You cannot drink from my fountain. You are different.

The water is only sweet to me.
You cannot drink from my fountain.
Your skin is different, your face is different than mine. It will taste bitter to you.

You cannot drink from my fountain.
You are not as intelligent as I, you are not my equal.
I have turned it off.

You cannot have water from my fountain.
I do not care if you thirst.
I do not care if you die.

My fountain has run dry.
It does not work.
May I have some water?

Yes, you may have some water from my well.
Take as much as you want.
I care.

The Road

A burst of light and there is a sunrise on a new life.
The rays cast a glow over a new road.
The end disappears at the far horizon.

It leads to the avenues of life as the sun brightens.
Twisting and turning it leads us onward.
Forward it leads us to triumphs and troubles, new lives and hope.

As we travel potholes and cracks appear.
It ages and fades with time and worry.
Hope and lives fade.

Overhead the sun dims.
It meets the road at the horizon.
The road becomes a shadow, the world grows dark; it is sundown.

Self-Sacrifice

Life makes me bleed.
But I will help even though it hurts.
I will endure even though I suffer.

I will not be broken.
I will continue to help others.
I will always be there with a helping hand.

I can be consumed with hate.
But I will not repeat it to others.
I will show compassion.

Anger can swell in me like a storm.
But I will control it.
I will not cause anger in others.

I will sacrifice myself for others.
I will sacrifice myself so that others will not sorrow.
I will sacrifice myself for my family because it is my everything.

To Touch the Sky

Our world is hollow.
Our world is ingrained with hate.
Our world is inherent with fear.
Our world is rife with anger.

We stomp for pleasure.
Staring down at the broken.
Grinning at what we have done.
Hoping it will cause fear until all is lost.

Only at the precipice do we help for pleasure.
Reaching down to those who are broken.
Helping up those who are in fear.
To support and help the trodden.

A tear drops when we hate.
A tear drops when we love.
We must reach upward.
We can raise up.

We weep for the past.
We must look up.
We must cry out for our future.
We can touch the sky.

Hand, Mind, and Heart

A hand, a mind, and a heart. What a creation they are.
In a cool calmness, they create sublime sounds and sublime words.
Or, terrible sadness.

With a clenched fist they can create anger or joy.
They can draw out a deep love for all or a hatred to end all.
They can give for all, help all, or destroy everything.

On the darkest of dark nights.
A blackness so unrelenting that no flicker of love can penetrate it.
But a helping hand can turn it into a brilliant glow of life.

Heart can bring a tear to the eye.
Wipe away that tear.
And it can change the world.

One at a time they can struggle.
One at a time they can lose focus.
In concert the world trembles at their strength.

The outstretched hand.
The glow of a warm heart.
The care of a giving mind all are the soul of life.

Photographs and Memories

Hearts and souls are captured.
Hearts and souls are remembered.
Hearts and souls that will be cherished, forever.

Photographs of times long past.
Photographs of when we were young.
Pictures of what once was.

Memories of all the times spent together in happiness.
Memories that will always be there in a quiet moment.
Of love and warmth and a good laugh.

Photographs and memories make life never-ending.
A story to be remembered.
A story of a life to never be forgotten. There is never an end.

Rain

Skies darken as the rain falls.
Spirits become sullen and lose heart.
But life moves forward.

Endless is the rain.
Never ceasing, always falling.
But the world carries on.

Rain causes the roots of life to grow.
Rain is the need of life.
Rain is the cause of life.

The rain passes.
A brilliant blue arcs across the sky.
A life-giving glow caresses the soul.

The soul grows into a new life.
The soul smiles at what is ahead.
At what it has learned from the rain.

The Unknown

There is an eternal memory in a tomb of the strongest stone.
Stone hewn out of the very ground from which a life was born.
A life that stands for freedom and Liberty.

A gentle wind breathes softly over the tomb.
Within, valor and honor cry proudly.
The breeze speaks to all who will listen.

A lone guard stands in silence before the stone.
The immovable protector defends against the foolish and unwise.
A guard who is a symbol of a country.

The guard walks slowly, quietly, with reverence.
Over and over, he retraces his steps.
As quiet as the breath of wind that caresses the stone.

1117

From now on you do not have a name.
Your number is 1117.
Do not forget your number.

My life is over.
A new life has been forcibly installed.
What can I do? What can we do?

I am surrounded by utter despair.
Around me is only fear.
Aimlessly, downcast multitudes slog by me.

What do I do? I do what they say or the ultimate end.
1117 must do what they say.
1117 must do what it hears.

But, 1117 still has its dignity.
But, 1117 still has its honor.
But, 1117 will still help those in need.

1117, I, will not bow to the force above me.
1117, I, will sacrifice myself for others.
I will not live the way the rule demands I do.

My name is not 1117.
I will not be what someone else wants me to be.
I am me. I will be me.

Whispers

An enigmatic voice from the dark, whispers in an ear.
It speaks of riches, glory, and power. Power to buy friends.
Riches to buy wealth. Glory to buy rewards.
But the whisper is a lie.

The whisper grows. It passes from ear to ear, turning it from the truth.
Eyes light up, with hope for an easy life.
The whisper asks only to be listened to.
To be the leader for life without strife.

Families sprout with the lie for a companion. It lives with them,
directing its biding.
Fathers and mothers teach the young. The lie gains a foothold in the future.
Children learn from the whispers' teachings.
They teach their friends, corrupting the innocent. Race comes forth,
perpetuating an idea.
Greed swells, filling the pockets with gold. Hatred screams
as it comes into its own.

The whisper turns into cannon shot in crowds.
It races from ear to ear, instantly changing the good.
The crowd moves like one living mass.
Changing and morphing into evil.

Good speaks softly, but with unrelenting force.
It stands its ground against evil, dreaming of harmony and freedom.
Fathers and mothers teach the young.
Good speaks of peace, serenity, and the bravery of life.

Love and knowledge spring from that life.
Knowledge fathers dreams, dreams that build the future.
It pushes the evil away. Transformed they follow path of love.
The evil cowers in the corner, where it waits patiently again.

Parents

They love and respect us.
Cajole and deny us.
Clean and clothe us.

And, they will always be there.

They teach us and guide us.
Cause us to remember and forget.
Teach us the difference between right and wrong.

And, they will always be there.

When they are not there.
When they are not here.
We know and remember that they will always be there.

When

When will we stop?
When will we stop fighting?
When will we stop killing?
When will we start living?

Aggression leads to aggression.
Fear leads to fear.
Hate leads to hate.
When do we...

Anger fosters fear.
Fear fosters anger.
Hate leads to aggression.
Aggression leads to killing.

When the killing stops will there be anyone left?
When the hate stops will there be anyone left to hate?
When fighting stops will there be anyone living?
When do we...

When do we start living?
When do we start growing?
When do we start?
When do we...when?

True Friends

These are my friends. My friends.
Matoskah, White Bear, the proud Native American.
Juan, the guitar player from Puerto Rico.
Rick the farmer's son. Sean from the Bronx, Bob from Texas.
And I, Staff Sergeant Rick.

I have been through hell with them.
They have been through hell with me.
Wounds are treated like insults. Anger is returned.
We are the best when it is the worst.
We fight for our country. We fight for the honor to do so.

No one will stop us from defeating the enemy.
No one will come between me and my friends.
Many have fallen without a second word; others die in screams.
I have killed. We have killed. We do our jobs. Indifference blinds our memories.

Forward, always forward. We are tired of walking. When will it end?
When will we go home? It is cold. It is hot. It is always raining.
The mud sticks to our boots like a mass of leeches.
The bugs. The bugs. More and more bugs.

Artillery shells rain down on our foxholes.
Men disappear in a roar.
Even though we are brave we cower in our homes in the ground.
It feels like the safety of 'home', the only memory we have left.

A deafening roar. Help me! I am hit.
Blood oozes from my chest. My friends surround me.
White Bear presses a bandage onto the gaping wound.
They tell me to hang on.

The world around me grows dim.
Their voices become slow mumbles.
The world goes dark.
I am alive. I am home.

The Price of Immortality

I want to live forever.
I never want to die.
I want to feel and see everything, to be everything.
I am afraid to die.

The process is done.
Done secretly, against my wife's wishes, I am now immortal.
Euphoric is weak for an explanation, humbling insignificant.
My wife and children have left me, but I am still alive.

I have been in several test accidents and survived.
Nothing can touch me.
I can do anything, bad.
Laws of Man and God do not apply to me.

Death and destruction I have left in my wake.
Secretly starting wars, plagues, and famine I watch millions.
I still survive. The smile on my face aches.
I feel glorious.

Years creep along. I have lost track of time.
All I have known, all I have needed, is gone.
The world is cold and dark. Snow falls constantly.
Winds blow unmercifully, unceasing.

My smile dissolved centuries ago replaced by one of indifference.
I do not care as I trudge through the deep snow.
I do not feel the cold; its stinging bite has no teeth.
I do not want to feel anymore.

The sun, though high overhead, is stunted.
Dull it is, its life-giving warmth long since faded.
Mankind has long since gone.
I am alone on my world, my world of loneliness.

It is my perfect barren world.
Nothing changes.
Nothing moves but the snow and the relentless bitter wind.
Images of my wife and children have long since faded.

There is nothing in the future.
The past distant beyond my now feeble imagination.
I want to die.
Will I die? Help me, God.

The Joy of Music

Stand in triumph.
Listen to the mind burst forth.
Fill the chest; learn what the heart is saying.

Watch the eyes brighten and tear.
Feel the rhythm pound the chest.
Touch the wood, feel its power to guide.

Pull the bow 'cross the strings.
Listen to the senses waft skyward.
Let them fly.

Caress the ivory.
Create the strength; let the notes rise to fill the air with love.
Let the arms close and embrace the passion.

Entice the voice from the soul.
Lure it from the depths and send it bursting forth.
Send the dream of music to the mountaintop and over the land.

Music knows no boundaries.
It has no borders.
It is timeless, limitless.

No language can stop it.
Hatred cannot prevent it.
It is forever.

Bruce A Humphrey

Resolve

I must have the resolve to say, 'I will not!'
The resolve to say, 'They will not!'
No one will say to me, 'You will change your life to suit me.'
'You will change your life to serve me.'

I must have the resolve to do whatever I wish.
To live where I wish, to grow a family, and to survive.
A shattered peace in the world, a shattered peace in America, we will not falter.
People have died but there is no submission, resolve does not falter.

Destruction is not absolute.
The spark of resolve builds to a blaze and rebuilds the broken lives.
The eyes of the dazed and bloodied turn to rage, we have not changed.
We will do as we wish.
Justice comes in many forms and will come.

Sanity and insanity are bedfellows.
Screaming ideas and ideologies they try to break each other's resolve.
But resolve is the backbone of life, of civilization.
We must use it to stop them; we will use it to live.

I will not do as they want, I will never do what they need.
I will not do what they need, which is to fester, slither and spread their dark ideas.
I will do as I want, I will do as I need.
Thank the peaceful Gods for my choice.

Why We Never Forget

Teary eyes twinkle in the morning light as a body is carried past.
Another young life whose heart has stopped beating.
Another young scared child who overcame a brutal fear and defended
the country.

A single second in time and they are gone.
A moment in eternity and they but memories in our hearts.
Memories of happiness and of a beloved home.

Fathers and mothers hold each other tightly for comfort but it does
not bring back their child.
Siblings try to understand but cannot.
'Why?' they say. 'Who did?' they say.

But the country they died defending still stands strong due to them.
Our hearts are saddened for what they had to endure for us.
Our hearts bleed for their sacrifice.

A mother and father lay a rose on the child's chest.
The child does not see it, does not move to grasp it. The child
will never move again.
The child will never look into their sad soulful eyes again.

But, deep down, the parents are proud. Their heads are held high.
Their child will forever be a hero.
A hero that came forth when the need was greatest.

Their child will never be forgotten.
Never will the child be lost to time.
Their country will never be alone.

Man

Life begins in the heavens. Drifting down, it lies on the earth until the rain brings it into being.

Growing gently, it spreads over the land until every corner is screaming, Here I am!

The man then caresses the flower of life, nurturing it, teaching it the way of the future.

He creates and builds cities akin to the mountain and the river.

He pushes his way over the prairie and the water making a way for his future.

He cares for the young and elderly to preserve his way of life, for all mankind.

Reaching, stretching his fingers to the limit he explores the depths of the oceans.

Or, the infinities of the sky.

His imagination delves into the unknown seeking out the truth of life, for all mankind.

War makes man the beast. Jealousy, hatred, racism, man creates all this within himself to keep the balance.

At times he kills indiscriminately, callously, to create fear and anger, furthering his goal.

He longs for the sweet taste of power not realizing the ending bitterness.

Yet, he will reach out with a helping hand to catch the falling, keep the sick from dying, and to teach the living.

Man's mind is boundless.

It is capable of creating or destroying a single cold thought.

It is unchangeable and changeless.

Mystical and methodical, it can move his mountains or go to the stars.

But with a single spoken or written word, it can stop the world, for all mankind.

Love

It is late, and the room is dark. I am alone.
My heart hums softly.
Quiescent in its dull slumber, it drums slowly, unaffected.
With my head on the pillow, I can hear and feel my blood.

Thump... thump... thump.
It pumps leisurely, unhurried in its attempt to keep me from slumber.
Eyeing a white blank wall, I wait.
Silence has command of the room.

Wind in the outside world causes the house to creak, the windows to rattle.
The room remains still.
A random desire floats out of the black mist of my mind.
A woman's face, a delicate face, intercedes; eyes staring, all in my mind.

The face begins to smile, small and gentle.
The power of the face dissolves the wall until only the face remains.
Sounds of surging blood I can hear now.
Thumping, drumming, coursing.

My breathing becomes heavy, and my true feelings are released.
A smile draws across my trembling lips. A heaviness settles in my chest.
Warm and pleasant the feeling crushes the silence.
The room glows with excitement. I am alive. I feel no pain or loneliness
for I am in love.

Imagination

From the birth of humankind arises the miracle of imagination.
From the creation of fire to the conception of the artificial mind.
In our infancy, we first beheld the sun in the heavens.
In our infancy, we saw the orb that is Earth from orbit.

When we gaze into our newborn's eye we see the creation of our
human empires.
The baby's hand reaches outward and we hold it, comforting it as it grows.
The baby's adventure of exploring, seeking, and knowing the utter beauty
of learning forces it onward.

It fights to caress what he touches.
Its wants and needs are nourished and inspired.
Its ideas can turn the smallest grain of matter into utter destruction
or indescribable beauty of existence.

The flower blossoms signal the adult coming of age.
Stretching, and reaching, it moves out into the world.
Tapping life on the shoulder it longs to help but in its way.

Sculpting his likeness in the past he longs for eternity.
Probing the future he ignores the past.
Forever living, forever changing, forever growing, the mind's eye can
awaken the universe.

I Am

I am the world; I live in unending change.
Moving, growing, and dying.
My surface, wiped clean by man, is refreshed by my gentle touch.

I am Man, changeless, unsympathetic, and cruel.
Forever changing, forever loving, forever growing.
I am both willful and subject to leadership.
I judge with a simple look, that judgment is slow to change.

I suffer as a blade slices the soul dissecting it into good and evil.
I know no bounds, I touch everyone, everything.
I bring humans together and rip them apart.

I am holocaust the absolute; I do nothing but endure and die.
Faces mean nothing, hearts are blank and sterile.
The end and beginning are one.

I am harmony.
The rose and thorn are my playmates.
Snow-capped mountains and golden plains are my children.
I live in the heart of man.

Fear

Fear drives the world.
Fear of doing, fear of not doing.
Fearful to live, fearful to die.

Fear believes in not enough; fear believes in too much.
Fear feeds the flame of going too far.
And feeds off the need of not going far enough.

Fear cannot look into its own eyes.
It cannot see itself in the mirror.
Fear is blind to itself.

Fear serves the furrowed brow.
Serves the drive that is anger.
Serves the anger that is fear.

Fear drives the need to love.
And drives the need for power.
It needs hatred.

Fear prowls the street looking for followers.
It derives its courage from others.
It derives its strength from the many.

It draws in the hopeless.
Draws in the directionless.
Fear attracts itself.

Fear is enraged by courage.
Causing it to lose power.
It has no power in the face of strength.

Courage builds from the strength of light.
The strength of hope.
The strength of resolve.

Courage and Fear merge.
Fear and Courage derive strength from one another.
Courage and Fear are, man.

Dawn

Step, step, step.
Dawn, motion, life takes the first step.
Quick-paced and looking forward is the spirit of energy.

Eyes open onto a bright world full of wonder, full of excitement.
Deep blue skies arc above.
Tapestries of light and dark nurture the land.

Growing older, the eyes become more aware.
Seeing more dark than light an eye tears.
Love wears away the innocence, making them intense.

Step, step . . . step.
Time advances unceasingly, widening the eyes.
They see life distorted.

Trials in life make them steely, hard.
Time paces out the last steps.
Twilight transforms the eyes, once alive with spirit, to weary and cynical.

The rhythm of time is deliberate the steps move toward an end.
The lids descend. Step, step, step.
Life's enchantment commences again.

Bright and cheerful, it reaches for the light above.
A raging, burning fire of hope seeks the hidden secrets.
A life begins, a life ends, and such is the way of life.

Civil Warriors

Standing with my comrades, I look across the battlefield and see a brother.
He is not my friend; he is the enemy.
Why? For my future? For our future? For his future?
But I must. For what? The future?

Terrified inside, proud outside.
Comrades, lead me, hold my hand bolster my heart.
My first step is excruciating, but I must go.
Steady, steady, step, step, stronger, stronger, faster, faster.
Death whispers at my ear, but I do not hear it. It stares into my eyes, but I do not see it.

Pride pushes me forth, blinding me to the fear.
Staccato sounds erupt, something sizzling comes close.
Men drop like wheat before the scythe.
My friends, my comrades, all are dying.

A burning pain grips my chest, searing, searing.
My coat turns red, my hands turn red.
I, I fall, to the waiting Earth.
My eyes see a friend die horribly, a comrade, a brother.

Fury ceases the burn.
Rising up I charge forward, I must, I must.
Charge, charge, kill, kill.
More pain, more agony, more red.
Why? Why, for my future, for my future.

Children

They inherit the wind.
They inherit our souls.
They will believe in us.
They are us.

Why do we not cherish them?
Why do we not protect them?
Why do we not love them?
Why are they not...?

We are teachers.
We are leaders.
We are their hearts.
We are their beginning.

When do we stop?
When do we start?
When will we believe?
When do we know?

What do we do when...?
What do if they are left...?
What do we do when they are...?
What do we do when...?

Children bring us to the brink of our future.
Children bring us to understanding.
Children bring us to the mirror.
Children bring us home.

Canyons of the Mind

Deep they are.
Chasms deep, seemingly bottomless, hold despair within them.
Despair, born from ineptness, breeds and grows.

It boils in the darkness, yet has no shape.
Roiling and bubbling, it creates nothing.
Blackened by ignorance it pulls all down with it.

Walls are slick, offering no aid.
The ceiling, a pinpoint of light, offers little to hope.
Smells within the canyons are odorless; the air, sterile.

Yet, the hope of friendship keeps the point of light from fading.
The heart, at one time sobbing, beats heavily with hope.
Happiness has not been forsaken.

A foothold appears against the wall, though small, it is a beginning.
A hand appears in the darkness.
A helping hand?

Bony pale fingers stretch forth, reaching.
Drifting closer to hope they strengthen and become young.
Full with the strength of love, they guide hope toward the foothold.

Cautious, the first step is cautious.
The sides of the canyons are steep.
Careful, careful.

Hope climbs the canyon wall.
The vaporous form pulls free of the seething mess.
The hand rests on hopes back for reassurance.

The pinpoint of light overhead grows brighter.
It reveals a face on the vapor, it is strong.
The canyon walls become less steep.

A ledge appears above.
The helping hand dissolves.
Strength in the vapor resounds in the canyon.

The light is now blinding.
It binds the vapor to the strength.
The canyon wall falls away.

The vapor is now alive.
It stands strong and firm on the good earth.
The sun reveals the face it is, us.

Alone

I did not see it; therefore, it did not happen.
I did not see the death of one.
I did not witness the extermination of millions.
I did not write the history; therefore, it is false.
I will not believe what I did not write.

I did not sanction a soldier to die for me; I am free on my own accord.
I do not see the sacrifice of millions or feel the pain of their suffering.
I did not cry for lost.
I will not cry for those I did not know.
I did not hear it; therefore, it did not occur.

I need not be grateful for those who came before me.
I need not be grateful to those who greeted me with freedom.
I need no one to guide me through life.
I ask no one for help with the inequities of living.
I will not acknowledge the assistance for my way of thinking.
I did not ask for help, therefore I am myself.

I am me.
I am not lonely.
I need no one for help or love.
I love nothing for there is nothing to love.
I am not emotional, therefore I need no one.

I am isolated from humanity.
I am isolated from myself.
I, therefore, am not allowing myself to feel.
I will not feel for those who died before me.
I will not grieve for the sacrifice others have made for me. I will remain lonely.

Heart

Born is the heart, full of life, vigor, and dreams.
There are no hatreds, feelings of hostility or fears.
It beats gently, driving life through the corridors of flesh as it grows.

Nurtured it grows with the soft embrace of love.
Pumping freely, never ceasing, it sees only the future.
Hope and freedom are forever entwined on its soul.

It must defend itself against the ideals which would tear it apart.
It must shield itself from despair, harden its soul.
Courage and faith bring it strength.

It beats strong with the knowledge of life, forever learning, forever growing.
Perpetually it drives understanding and devotion outward.
It thrives on warmth and understanding.

It does not know the barriers of language.
It does not recognize the bigotry of color.
It does not listen to the unswerving devotion to a single ideal, shutting out all others.

As age encroaches upon it the heartbeat slows.
Knowledge of life is no longer able to sustain it.
The embrace of love begins to fade.

The warmth of hope and freedom chills.
The heart begins a slow-motion fall into the abyss.
Toward the light of happiness and everlasting peace.

Heros

For all those who did not come home.
For all those who cannot feel a warm breeze again.
For all those whom we cannot touch, again.

For all those who we cannot embrace again.
For all those, we cannot love again.
For all those who cannot live again.

We thank you. We revere you and your courage.
We kneel before you and raise our hearts to you.
We feel your pain, those who cannot be again.

We look into eyes only in our memories.
We grieve for thee, those who cannot.
We bow our heads in love.

We live because of you.

Veterans Day

Can you stand against a 50-caliber bullet?
Can your skin repel white phosphorous or a nerve gas?
Can your body withstand a flamethrower, grenade or bayonet?

Those who fight our wars deserve to be recognized.
We do this every year as not to forget. Honor them as they honor us.
We give them praise as they do for us for our support.

They travel far from home, away from their families.
Traveling to all corners of the Earth separated from their loved ones.
By land, by sea, and air they journey into danger and solitude.

Dark it is. Midnight. Nothing but the insects chirping their songs.
Suddenly, roars of explosions. Men scream. Men die.
Men in holes hold their own against onslaught after onslaught.

Men come home. Some do not.
People wait, then smile and cheer.
People wait and wait then walk away. There is nothing to cheer for here.

For their valor we are alive. Our lives go on as they have.
Our children grow without interference from those who would take our freedom.
Our Freedom reigns supreme. Freedom is beyond doubt alive.

A Question to Humanity

Why are only one people mourned in history?
Did it begin with man subjugating man?
Is there an underlying difference in the essence of the soul?
Is there a difference between the subjugated and the subjugators?

What puts one race that persecutes above the persecuted?
What brings it to the forefront?
Is it documentation, the power of the written word or the photograph?
Is it the weapons they are slaughtered with?

Are we not all humans? Under the skin are we not all equal to all others?
What makes one human more important than the other?
Is it the fear that we all have that if we don't submit, we will die?
Once the strong have the upper hand why do they try to control others?

Does it all boil down to our basic instinct of survival?
Is it the terrifying fact that death is at the doorstep if one does not submit?
Is it simply those who think they are strong but actually weak?
Are they simply trying to build their courage?

The only answer, there are no answers.
Anger, fear, and the basic survival instinct halt intelligent thought.
Beneath all the languages and technologies, we are still, savages.

Those Who Come Home

I am sorry, I cannot use my arms, but I can work.
I am sorry, I cannot use my legs, but I can work.
I am sorry, I cannot see, but I can work.
I am sorry, I am a little jittery, but I can work.
Please, can you give me a job? Please, I need a job.

I am sorry you cannot use your arms; we have nothing for you.
I am sorry you do not have any legs. We need you to stand for long hours.
I am sorry you cannot see. All of our work is visual.
I am sorry that you are not stable, but you have to interact with others.
I am sorry; we do not have a job for you.

I cannot reach into my pocket for bus fare; someone is kind and helps,
then steals it.
I cannot roll in the snow; the tires of my wheelchair keep slipping.
I cannot see. My touch stick hits a curb. I step off and a car nearly hits me.
The driver screams.
I cannot talk to others because I get angry. I sit alone in the corner of
a restaurant.

My hand is out hoping someone will take it and help.
My hand is out for help, not sympathy.
My hand is out reaching for life.
My hand is out, hoping for a smile.

A Voice in the Wind

Summits, valleys, pulsing rhythms, the magical whisper of life is on the wind.
Wafting, screaming, shaping silhouettes, its serene touch moves the
world unceasingly.
Crashing seas bring forth new changes, mysterious and deadly.

A new age arises stretching to the sun.
A challenge grows in the wind, seeds drop and life begins.
Strengthening, the wind turns into a raging river until one voice is heard,
the voice of man.

The thunderous voice strives to change the present, shape the future,
and preserve it.
Majestic unmovable mountains wane.
Bowing to the voice they shudder and shake, finally crumbling to dust.

Seas vast, deep, and mysterious are traversed, used by the voice, and tamed.
The land, broken and altered by man's mind, submits to the revolution.
A new eon has begun.

Soldiers at Rest

Sit; listen to the silence.
Sit; listen to the valor.
Rest, and listen to the whisper of the wind.

The wind carries the message.
The message is honor.
Honor is remembrance.

The past bristles with dignity.
Dignity bristles with strength and courage.
Sons, daughters, husbands, and wives, forever rest in a sea of grace.

Tears flow, salutes are crisp and rigid.
Valor and honor are laid to rest.
Alone they are not, forgotten they are not.

We stand beside them and bow our heads.
We sit next to them and look skyward.
We love, we respect, and we humble ourselves in their presence.

The thunder of silence echoes through the hills.
The silence of a passing, the thunder of valor is remembered.
Unknowns they are not, forever being in our hearts.

The wind carries the whisper.
Whispers carry the message.
The message is the silence of respect.

Sit; listen to the silence.
Sit; listen to the valor.
Rest, and listen to the whisper of the wind.

The Missing Man

A young, terrified soldier lies in the dirt fighting a useless war.
He hides from the raging battle; he hides from his fear.
Friends die to the left; a friend dies to the right.
What to do, what to see, where to go, what to fight.

Unseen enemies hurl death in his direction.
Bits of earth are tossed into the air.
A weapon is gripped tightly in hand.
Should he, should he?

Through the darkness, he sees friends die.
Bursts of white reveal flashes of red.
His ears ring from the near-constant detonations.
Can he, can he.

Another flash. Another thunderous crash.
Dirt splatters on his face, choking him.
He's had enough. Anger crushes his fear,
He crawls from the pit.

Around and over, over and through, he crawls.
He readies himself,
Pulling the weapon into position, he aims.

He sees a face, a face in the flashes.
The face sees him, fear resurges.
Quick, quick. Do it, do it.
Triggers are pulled, more flashes, more flashes.

For an instant; silence overtakes the scene.
A quiet in the chaos. Then a telltale moaning of injured men, and dying boys.
On a small hill, a young man's life drains into the dirt.
A young, frightened hero.

At home, a favorite chair is empty.
At the funeral, a coffin is draped with a symbol.
People gather to remember, grieve, and console.
Overhead a trio of jets roars. One is missing, the symbol. The missing man.

Good and Evil

An enigmatic voice from the dark whispers in a naïve ear, it speaks of riches, glory, and power.
Riches to buy wealth, glory to buy rewards, power to buy friends, but the whisper is a lie.
It grows passing from ear to ear turning it from the truth, eyes light up with hope for an easy life.
The whisper asks only to be listened to, to be the leader for a life without strife.

Families sprout with the lie for a companion.
It lives with them, directing its bidding.
Fathers and mothers teach the young.
The lie now has a foothold on the future.

Children listen to the whisper's teachings, learning from them.
They teach their friends, who tell theirs, corrupting the innocent.
Race comes forth, perpetuating an idea.
Greed swells, filling the pockets with gold, hatred screams as it comes into its own.

The whisper turns into a cannon shot in crowds.
It races from ear to ear, instantly changing those who are good.
The crowd moves like one living mass changing and morphing into evil.
But the one who says, 'I will not' stands its ground.

Good speaks softly but with unrelenting force.
Unmoving against evil, it dreams of harmony and the legacy of freedom.
Fathers and mothers teach the young.
Good speaks of peace, serenity, and the bravery of life.

Love and knowledge spring from that life.
Knowledge fathers dreams, dreams that build the future.
It drives the evil away from the naïve forcing it back into the dark corner, where it cowers and waits once again.
The naïve are transformed and sent on the path of love once more.

Hands

Remarkable hands, storied hands.
Hands, hands can build.
Hands can mold, shape, and speak.
Hands can grasp for the heavens, touch it, and believe in the make believers.

Through the fingers, thoughts explode as pen touches paper.
Tones and melodies erupt from inner emotions becoming reality.
Heart and soul become one as fingers scrawl quickly, feverishly.
Pounding blood surges through the fingers forcing the pen onward,
causing tears to fall from an eye.

Truth flows from the mind; the hand transports it into being.
Embracers of the brush, digits move carefully following intricate lines drawn
on canvas.
Colors blend together, vibrant, beautiful, soaring to mosaics of sky and water.
The calming sense of touch slows the scene until order graces the fabric.

Forgotten until they are lost.
Forgotten until they are crippled, hands are taken for granted for their
life-giving talent.
Bent and crooked they are silenced from the song they once sang.
Memories now distant are relegated to the wall or museums.
Dusty shelves house the books of the once pulsating, vital, movements that
the hand generated.

Hands have saved lives and taken them just as easily.
They create the saviors of life as well as the purveyors of death.
Creating and destroying with a single move a finger can move mountains
or search the unknown heavens.

Hands live to caress and love.
Hands live to fight and die.
Forever living hands, forever exploring are hands.